Step-by-Step

Printing

Michelle Powell

Search Press

First published in Great Britain 2000

Search Press Limited
Wellwood, North Farm Road,
Tunbridge Wells, Kent TN2 3DR

Reprinted 2001, 2004

Text copyright © Michelle Powell 2000

Photographs by Search Press Studios
Photographs and design copyright © Search Press Ltd. 2000

ISBN 0 85532 911 4

Suppliers
If you have difficulty in obtaining any of the materials and equipment mentioned in this book, then please visit the Search Press website for details of suppliers: www.searchpress.com

Alternatively, you can write to the Publishers at the address above, for a current list of stockists, which includes firms who operate a mail-order service.

Acknowledgements
The Publishers would like to thank Bridgeman Art Library for permission to reproduce the photograph on page 5.

This book is dedicated with love to Doris Winifred Powell

With special thanks as always to Jon, Mum and Dad for all their help and support. Many thanks also to the wonderful team at Search Press, and thanks to Gemma.

* * * * * * * * * * * * * * * *

The Publishers would like to say a huge thank you to Natalie Sawyer, Rupert Malins, Michael de la Bédoyère, Daisy Browne, Jeremy Thornby, Jessika Kwan, Natasha Nokes, Henry Sparshott, Elizabeth Pentacost, Letitia Thomas, Daniel Brisefer, Lucia Brisefer and Abu Subhan.

Finally, special thanks to Southborough Primary School, Tunbridge Wells.

When this sign is used in the book, it means that adult supervision is needed.

REMEMBER!
Ask an adult to help you when you see this sign.

Contents

Introduction

Printing is a process that involves making marks and reproducing those marks again and again. The marks can be shapes, patterns, pictures or words. Even a footprint in the snow is a basic form of printing.

The need for printing grew out of the need for written communication. Over five-and-a-half thousand years ago, the first writing appeared in Egypt as groups of symbols in clay tablets. As writing developed it was used to record events and re-tell stories. The ancient Egyptians wrote in pictures called hieroglyphics – one picture would represent a whole word or just part of a word. The Greeks, Romans, Vikings and other civilizations all had their own way of writing.

In the ninth century AD, the Chinese developed a method of printing using a carved wooden seal. They used this print to stamp official documents. Later, they produced carved wooden blocks to represent characters. The carved eraser stamps used in the dominoes project on pages 18–19 are made in a similar way.

Traditional printing methods are still used today. In this book I have looked at a variety of different techniques for making prints. The beauty of printing rather than drawing or painting, is that you can reproduce the same image over and over again, using the same printing block, tool or stamp. In this way you can quickly create a very detailed design with lots of repetition, or you can print on many items. This makes printing the perfect technique if you want to make lots of greetings cards for your friends, print up items to decorate your bedroom, or make unusual gifts for your family.

The first projects in the book use natural and man-made objects for printing. When you start looking for things to print with, you will soon discover that hundreds of different items are suitable. Cotton reels, scouring pads, bubblewrap, corrugated card, pen lids, corks and leaves can all be used to create interesting patterns and shapes.

I have also included projects which show different ways of creating printing blocks. You can use polystyrene, erasers, potatoes, string, foam and even pipe cleaners to make a fantastic range of designs. There are patterns at the back of the book that you can work from, or you can use your own drawings and designs to create unique prints.

Printing enables you to decorate many different things, and with a little experience you will soon be creating printed masterpieces of your own.

The most important thing of all is to have fun when printing!

You can take inspiration for your printing work from a number of different sources. It is often a good idea to draw out and paint your design first. This beautiful Egyptian design was first painted on to paper using an opaque watercolour paint called gouache. It was then made into a printing plate in about 1850 and used for printing textiles. It is not known who the artist was, but their design is now in the Design Library in New York, USA.

Materials

The items pictured on these pages are the basic tools and equipment you will need to start printing. You will already have most of them at home. Other items are easy to buy from local shops. In addition, there are some specific items needed for certain projects, such as magnets and sewing trim. You should check the list of materials carefully before you start each project.

Remember that whenever you use paints or glue, you should cover your work surface with newspaper or scrap paper. Wear old clothes and work on a tidy, flat surface. Have a damp cloth at the ready in case of spills. When you have finished printing, wash up your printing blocks in warm soapy water. Remember to also wash your printing block if you want to change colours when printing.

Water-based paint is used for most of the projects in this book. Acrylic or poster paints are the best to use. Special **fabric paint** is used when printing on material.

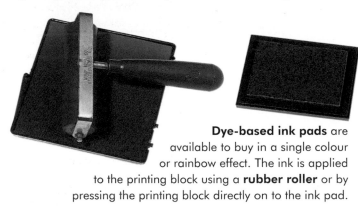

Dye-based ink pads are available to buy in a single colour or rainbow effect. The ink is applied to the printing block using a **rubber roller** or by pressing the printing block directly on to the ink pad.

Wallpaper paste is mixed in a **bowl** with **washing-up liquid** and paint to make a paste suitable for some printing.

Use an **iron** to fix any fabric paint. Iron on the reverse of the fabric when the fabric paint is dry. The heat from the iron will set the paint so that it will not disappear when the item is washed. Make sure an adult helps you iron.

Paintbrushes can be used to apply paint to printing blocks, and to add detail to printed items. A **sponge** or sponge roller can also be used to apply paint to a printing block.

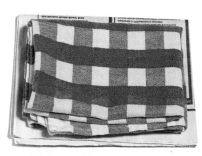

Printing is a messy craft and it is best to cover your work surface with **newspaper** or scrap paper before you begin. You should use a **cloth** to protect your ironing board when fixing fabric paints.

Thin card, cardboard, paper, clay, fabric and wood can all be printed on using the techniques in this book.

High-density foam can be cut out and stuck on to a block of wood to make a printing block. Cardboard is used to make a printing comb. Thin card or cardboard can also be used as a base for a printing block. Acetate, polystyrene, erasers, a potato, string and pipe cleaners can all be used to make different types of printing blocks. Patterned objects such as leaves, a scouring pad, sponges, bubblewrap and cotton reels can all be used to print with.

A lino cutter is used to carve a design in an eraser to make a printing block. Make sure you get an adult to help you when you do this.

A ruler is used for measuring and a ruler and pencil are used for drawing straight lines. A pencil can also be used to score polystyrene to make a printing block, and to transfer a pattern. A marker pen is used to mark out designs.

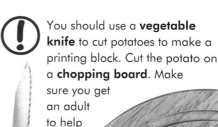

PVA glue is used to stick foam on to wood to make a printing block.

Scissors are used for cutting.

You should use a vegetable knife to cut potatoes to make a printing block. Cut the potato on a chopping board. Make sure you get an adult to help you.

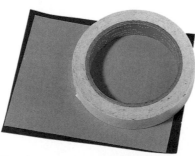

Tracing paper and carbon paper are used when transferring designs. The designs should be held in place with masking tape.

Natural Wrapping Paper and Gift Tag

YOU WILL NEED

Selection of leaves
Paper • Thin coloured card
Newspaper • Roller
Dye-based ink pad
String • Scissors
Hole punch

You can use many natural objects to print with. Look around the garden for flat stones and pieces of bark or ask for a slice of your favourite fruit or vegetable. This project uses a real leaf.

When choosing your leaf look for a flat, fresh one. Turn it over and feel the back. Leaves that have veins that you can feel are the best for printing. There are so many different trees to choose from – oak, maple, beech and sycamore to name a few.

2 Ink up the leaf using a rubber roller and a dye-based ink pad. Roll over the leaf a few times.

1 Choose a leaf with an obvious vein pattern.

3 Press the leaf firmly on to the paper. Smooth over it with your fingers.

4 Repeat the leaf pattern all over the paper. Leave to dry.

5 Cut out a rectangle of thin card and fold it in half to make a gift tag. Use a hole punch to make a hole in the folded edge.

6 Print a leaf on the gift tag. Loop a piece of string through the hole and tie to secure.

FURTHER IDEAS
Try using your leaf design on envelopes, writing paper, cards and invitations.

Sea Monster Game

The inspiration for this fun fishing game comes from the classical sea monsters which feature in the tales of Ancient Greek mythology. You can use textured objects such as bubblewrap and cotton reels to print your own double-headed sea serpents and giant squid. You will need small, round magnets to make this game. These are available from craft shops.

I have used seven sea monsters for this game, but you can make any odd number. For details of how to play the game, turn to page 29.

For details of how to play the game, turn to page 29.

YOU WILL NEED

Textured objects, e.g. bubblewrap, cotton reels, scouring pads, sponges
Thin card • Scrap paper • Newspaper
Tracing paper • Carbon paper
Masking tape • Water-based paint
Sponge roller • Paintbrush
7 paperclips • 2 magnets
2 pencils • Scissors
String

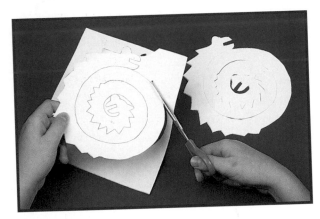

1 Transfer a mythical sea monster shape on to a piece of thin card (see pages 28–29). Cut it out. Repeat until you have seven sea monsters in total.

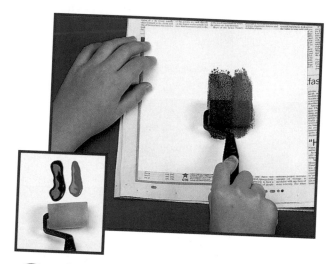

2 Place two stripes of different coloured paint on a piece of scrap paper. Run a sponge roller over both colours at once.

3 Choose a textured object such as bubblewrap, then use the roller to apply paint to one side of it. Turn the bubblewrap over then press it down on to the cut-out sea monster. Peel off to reveal the printed pattern. Leave to dry.

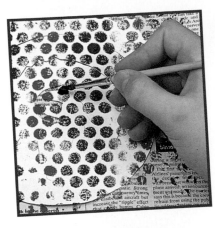

4

Continue, using different objects and colours, until all the sea monsters are decorated. Paint in the eyes then leave to dry. Repeat steps 2–4 on the back of all the sea monsters.

5

Attach a paperclip to the mouth of each sea monster.

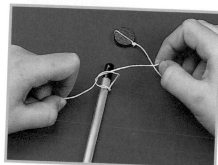

6

Tie a small magnet on to a piece of string. Tie the other end of the string on to a pencil. You are now ready to play the game.

FURTHER IDEAS

Tie your sea monsters to a coat hanger to create a colourful mobile.

Chinese Pencil Pot

If you are always losing your pencils and pens then this is the project for you. The pot is decorated with Chinese-style printed paper and gold trim is used to add the finishing touch.

A paint paste is spread thickly all over the paper then the design is created by scraping some of the paste away with a cardboard comb so that the paper shows through underneath. For best results use white paper and a darker coloured paint.

YOU WILL NEED

Cardboard tubing • Cardboard
Paper • Newspaper
Wallpaper paste • Washing-up liquid
Water-based paint • PVA glue
Small mixing bowl or dish
Paintbrush • Scissors
Length of trim

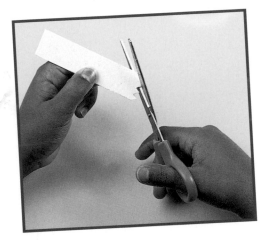

1 Use scissors to cut little V-shaped notches at one end of a small rectangle of cardboard to make a comb.

2 Mix up one cup of wallpaper paste with two teaspoons of paint and one teaspoon of washing-up liquid. Brush the paste mixture thickly on to your paper using a paintbrush.

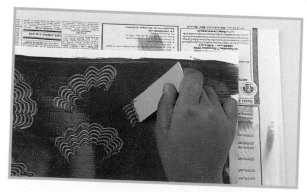

3 Use the cardboard comb to drag a pattern into the paste. Wipe the comb on some newspaper when it becomes clogged with paint.

4 Use a small strip of cardboard to add details. Work quickly before the paste dries. When finished, leave to dry.

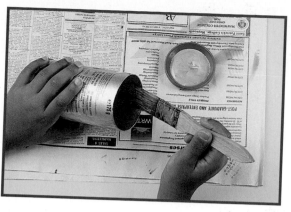

5 Cut the top off a length of tubing. Paint the inside to match your trim.

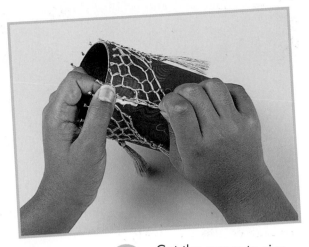

6 Cut the paper to size and glue around the side of the tubing to cover it. Finish by gluing a length of trim around the top.

FURTHER IDEAS

You can use this technique to cover a book or a small box.

Gecko T-shirt

The idea for this design comes from the paintings the Native American Indians used to decorate their tepees. I have chosen a gecko lizard for this T-shirt, but they painted many other designs. Some were used to encourage good spirits and fortunes. The paints they used were made from plants and soil, so the colours were natural and earthy.

This type of printing is called mono printing. Mono means 'one', and with this method of printing you can only make one print. This technique is ideal for transferring a colourful design on to fabric.

1 Transfer the gecko design shown on page 29 on to paper (see page 28). Place a sheet of acetate over the design and tape it in place.

2 Paint over one section of the design using one colour of fabric paint.

3 Turn the acetate face down on to the front of your T-shirt. Rub over the back of the acetate with your hand.

4 Carefully peel off the acetate. Touch up the colour with a paintbrush if necessary.

5 Repeat steps 1–4 with other colours to complete the design. Remember to line up the image carefully each time. When complete, leave the paint to dry thoroughly for twenty-four hours.

6 Turn the T-shirt inside out and place a piece of paper inside it. Iron over the design on the reverse side of the T-shirt. Ironing will fix the paints so that the colours do not come out when the T-shirt is washed.

(!) Make sure an adult helps you to iron the T-shirt.

FURTHER IDEAS
Use glow-in-the-dark paint to create a unique T-shirt.

Aztec Birthday Card

Bright, earthy colours and an Aztec sun design are used to create the Mexican theme for this original, hand-printed birthday card.

A piece of smooth, firm polystyrene (like that used for fast-food packaging) is used to create a printing block. This type of block can be used over and over again, so you can print lots of cards using the same design.

YOU WILL NEED

Coloured card • Polystyrene
Rainbow ink pad
Newspaper • Tracing paper
Carbon paper • Masking tape
Pencil • Scissors
PVA glue

1 Cut out a small square of polystyrene.

2 Transfer the sun design shown on page 29 on to the polystyrene (see page 28). Use a blunt pencil to score over the design.

3 Press the front of the polystyrene square on to a rainbow ink pad.

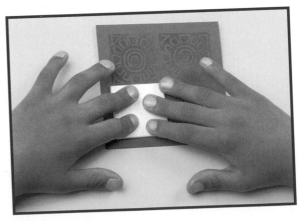

4 Press the polystyrene printing block into the corner of a piece of folded coloured card. Repeat in each corner.

5 Print the image on to a different coloured card, and then cut it out.

6 Glue the design into the centre of the folded card.

FURTHER IDEAS
You can decorate an envelope to match your card.

Egyptian Dominoes

The Ancient Egyptians used pictures called hieroglyphics to tell stories. Hieroglyphic designs are used in this project to create picture dominoes as a variation on the traditional dominoes game. For details about how to play the game, turn to page 30.

You can create wonderfully detailed printing blocks by carving a design into an eraser using a lino cutter. An eraser is soft enough to cut into easily and it transfers the paint well when you start printing.

For details about how to play the game, turn to page 30.

YOU WILL NEED

6 erasers • Lino cutter
Water-based paint • Paintbrush
Sponge • Coloured card
Newspaper • Tracing paper
Carbon paper
Pencil • Marker pen
Scissors • Ruler

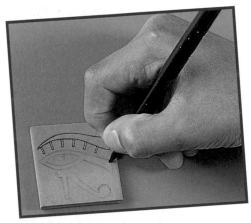

1 Transfer the six designs shown on page 30 on to six erasers (see page 28). Go over the outlines using a marker pen.

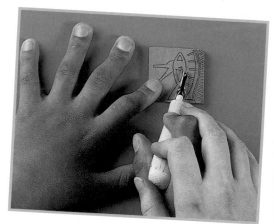

2 Use a lino cutter to carve out the areas around and within the designs. Cut with the blade pointing away, not towards you.

(!) A lino cutter is sharp. Make sure you get an adult to help you when you use it.

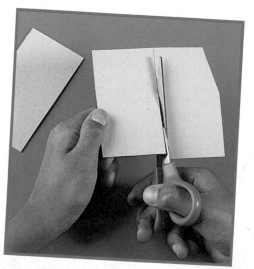

3 Use a ruler and pencil to mark out twenty-one identical rectangles on coloured card large enough to print two images on. Cut them out using scissors.

4 Use a sponge to apply paint to one of the designs on one of the erasers.

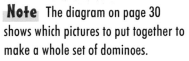

5

Press the eraser on to one end of one of the card rectangles. Repeat step 4 and continue printing. Make sure that each domino is different and that you have used each stamp six times.

Note The diagram on page 30 shows which pictures to put together to make a whole set of dominoes.

6

Add detailing to each of the designs using coloured paint and a paintbrush.

FURTHER IDEAS

Print one image on each piece of card. Make sure you have at least four of each design. Use these to play 'snap' with.

Modern Art Socks

You can get many great design ideas from looking at the work of modern artists. Try to recreate the colours and the patterns they have used. The designs in this project are inspired by the work of the French artist, Matisse.

Ordinary potatoes are used to print bold, lively images on to plain socks. Your potatoes will need to be quite fresh, so that they are still hard. Remember that the size of your design will be limited by the size of your potato.

1 Place one of your socks on a piece of thin card, then draw around it with a pencil. Cut out the shape.

2 Place the card template inside the sock.

(!) Vegetable knives are very sharp. Get an adult to help when you cut the potatoes.

3 Place two potatoes on a chopping board. Cut them in half using a vegetable knife.

4 Use a marker pen to copy the designs shown on page 31 on to the potatoes.

20

Get an adult to help you cut out the designs.

5 Use a vegetable knife to cut down around the edge of the design, then across from the side of the potato.

6 Paint over the raised designs with fabric paint, then print them on to your sock. Repeat all the steps to decorate the other sock. Iron to fix the colours (see page 15).

FURTHER IDEAS
You can decorate lots of items using this technique — baseball hats, canvas shoes or T-shirts, for example.

Mosaic Chalk Board

Mosaic designs are normally made by cutting glass or coloured tiles into small pieces then cementing them on to a wall or floor to create a picture or pattern. The Ancient Greeks and Romans are famous for mosaics.

In this project, a piece of high-density foam is cut into small squares and stuck to a wooden block. The block is then used to print instant mosaic designs. You could use thick cardboard instead of wood, but this means that you cannot wash and re-use the block. Before you begin, measure your chalk board and decide what size the designs need to be before you trace them from page 31.

before you trace them from page 31.

YOU WILL NEED

Chalk board
High-density foam
Square and rectangular wood off-cuts or thick cardboard
Water-based paints • Paintbrush
Newspaper • Carbon paper
Tracing paper • Masking tape
Pencil • Scissors
PVA glue

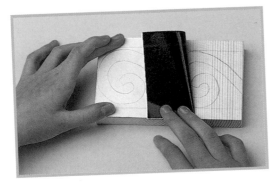

1 Transfer the designs shown on page 31 on to square and rectangular pieces of wood (see page 28).

2 Use scissors to cut a piece of high-density foam into small squares. Cut some of these squares into smaller, odd-shaped pieces.

3 Glue the square foam pieces on to each piece of wood, following the lines of the designs. Fill in the gaps with the small odd-shaped pieces of foam.

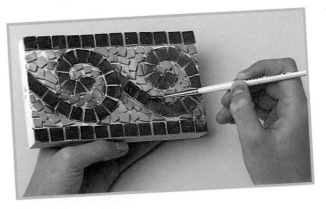

4 Paint over the raised foam images on both the square and rectangular printing blocks. Change colours where appropriate.

5

Press the square stamp on to one of the corners of the chalk board. Carefully lift the block off, apply more paint, then repeat at each corner.

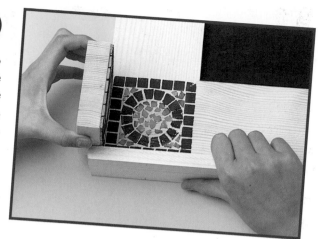

6 Print the rectangular block around the edge of the chalk board to create a border. Re-apply paint between each print.

FURTHER IDEAS
You can use this technique to decorate the rim of an indoor plant pot.

Asian Cushion

This sumptuous cushion is printed with a design inspired by traditional Asian arts. The design is known as paisley and is often used to decorate the elaborate saris worn by Asian women. In India and surrounding countries, very bright colours are popular for clothes and decorations.

The printing block for this project is made out of string glued to a piece of thin card. For best results choose string that is smooth, thick and quite stiff, as this will hold its shape well.

1 Transfer the paisley design shown on page 31 on to a piece of thin card. Cut it out, leaving a small border around the edge.

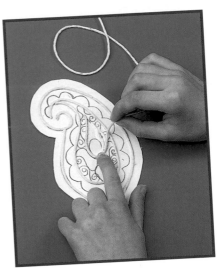

2 Glue string on to the card, following the line of the design.

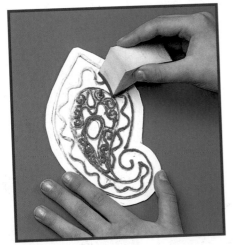

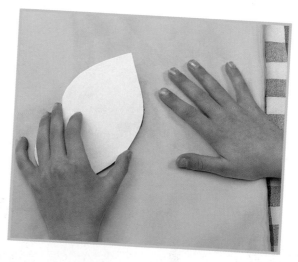

3  Apply fabric paint on to the string using a sponge.

4 Place the cushion cover on a smooth and soft surface such as a folded tea towel. This will make it easier to print the design. Press the painted side of the string design on to the plain cushion cover.

24

5

Repeat steps 3–4 all over the cushion cover, applying more paint to the string each time you make a print. Iron to fix the design (see page 15).

6 Place the cushion pad back inside the cover.

FURTHER IDEAS
You can use this technique to decorate a plain shoebag.

Primitive Clay Picture

The first recorded forms of art were the paintings on cave walls which were made by early settlers. The paintings usually showed images of men and animals and were painted in muted shades of red and brown. Like the Native American Indians, early settlers used soil and clay to create a type of paint.

You can create your own cave paintings by printing with pipe cleaners into air-drying clay. The clay is soft, so you can push the pipe cleaner shapes into the clay to leave an impression. When the clay has dried, it can be painted with earthy colours.

YOU WILL NEED

Air-drying clay
Pipe cleaners
Earthy-coloured water-based paints
Paintbrush • Sponge
Newspaper • Scissors

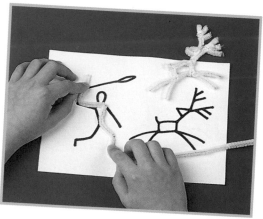

1 Photocopy and enlarge the pattern shown on page 31 (see page 28). Bend pipe cleaners to follow the lines of the designs.

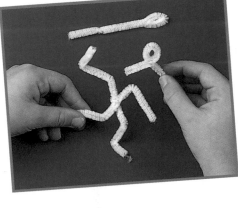

2 Work small sections at a time, cutting the pipe cleaners as you go. Join the pieces together by twisting them.

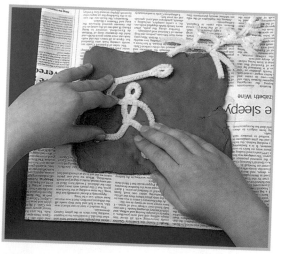

3 Press a piece of clay with your fingers to flatten it into a square shape.

4 Press the pipe cleaner designs into the clay to leave an impression. Remove them carefully then leave the clay to dry for twenty-four hours.

26

5 Sponge earthy-coloured paints randomly over the clay to create the effect of stone.

6 Use a paintbrush to paint around the shape of the designs so that they stand out.

FURTHER IDEAS
You can use this technique to make an unusual paperweight.

Patterns

You can trace the patterns on these pages straight from the book (follow steps 1–4). Alternatively, you can make them larger or smaller on a photocopier if you wish, and then follow steps 2–4.

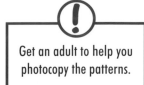

Get an adult to help you photocopy the patterns.

Transferring a pattern on to another surface

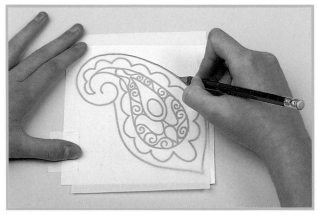

1 Place a piece of tracing paper over the pattern and then tape it down with small pieces of masking tape. Trace around the outline using a soft pencil.

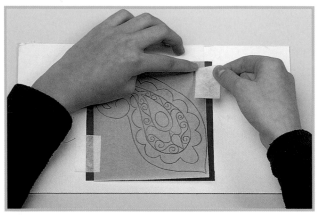

2 Place carbon paper on the surface you want to transfer the design on to. Place the tracing over the top and tape it in place.

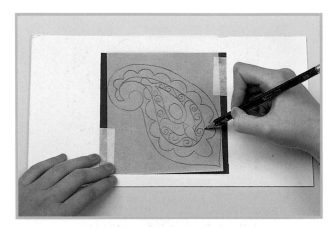

3 Trace over the outline with a pencil.

4 Remove the tracing paper and carbon paper to reveal the transferred image.

Patterns for the Sea Monster Game featured on pages 10–11.

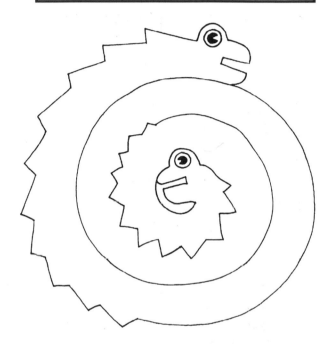

Rules for the Sea Monster Game
To play the game, pile up all the monsters, then use your pencil fishing rod to try and catch one. If you manage to lift it from the pile without entangling the others then you get to keep the monster. If not, put it back and let the next person have a turn. The winner is the person who has got the most monsters when the pile has gone.

Pattern for the Gecko T-shirt featured on pages 14–15.

Pattern for the Aztec Birthday Card featured on pages 16–17.

1 1	1 2	1 3	1 4	1 5	1 6
2 2	2 3	2 4	2 5	2 6	
3 3	3 4	3 5	3 6		
4 4	4 5	4 6			
5 5	5 6				
6 6					

The patterns shown below are for the Egyptian Dominoes featured on pages 18–19. They have all been given a number. Print your dominoes in the combinations shown here.

Rules for Dominoes

To play the game, deal each player seven dominoes face down. Leave the rest in a pile face down. Player 1 places a domino on the table; player 2 looks through their dominoes for a matching picture, and places that domino next to the first so that the pictures touch. Play continues in this way until a player cannot put a domino down. This player must pick up one of the spare dominoes and continue play. The winner is the first person to put down all of their dominoes. You can match two pictures at either end of the domino, and doubles can be played sideways.

1

2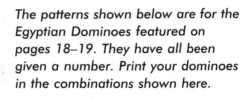

3

4

5

6

Pattern for the Asian Cushion featured on pages 24–25.

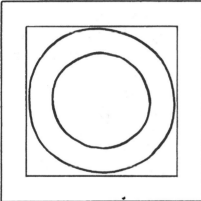

Patterns for the Modern Art Socks featured on pages 20–21. These cannot be transferred on to a potato using the technique shown on page 28, so you will need to copy them carefully yourself. Adjust the sizes according to the sizes of your potatoes.

Patterns for the Mosaic Chalk Board featured on pages 22–23.

Patterns for the Primitive Clay Picture featured on pages 26–27.

Index